Lounette Loubser, a South African author, holds a BA degree in Language and Culture, with Psychology and Linguistics as a double major. Her continued studies include Reiki and Art Therapy. Following a career in magazines and her contribution to Hans de Roos`s award-winning *Powers of Darkness: The Lost Version of Dracula,* Lounette published her debut novella *When Silence Speaks* in 2020.

Lounette Loubser

HELP!
MY MUM'S A WITCH

AUSTIN MACAULEY PUBLISHERS™
LONDON • CAMBRIDGE • NEW YORK • SHARJAH

A CIP catalogue record for this title is available from the British Library.

ISBN 9781398480315 (Paperback)
ISBN 9781398480322 (ePub e-book)

www.austinmacauley.com

First Published 2024
Austin Macauley Publishers Ltd®
1 Canada Square
Canary Wharf
London
E14 5AA

Thanks to my sister Pienette for showing me the door and to Zander for pushing me through it.

v

Help! My mom's a witch!

She tells me to pray for what I wish
every day,
And smokes the house to keep bad
things away.

She puts jars of water out
in the moon,
And sweeps her altar with an old
twiggy broom.

Mom's arms shimmer with bangles and rings.

In her hair, she'll put leaves, feathers and all sorts of things!

Our pantry is stocked with herbs
and shells,
Our front door jingles with
little bells.

At Halloween, when my friends beg
for candy,
I stay with Mom to light candles
for Granny.

When other kids have Christmas, we
have Yule,
Mom puts funny sigils in my
lunchbox for school.

Our house is filled with candles and dusty old books,
Mom even has a cauldron in which she cooks!

I don't understand why Mom does all
these things,
But it makes her smile, so she's
happy it seems.

At Beltane in springtime, with ribbons, we dance,
And Mom always wins when we play games of chance.

She tells me stories of old Gods
and new,
And shows me things about nature
that I never knew.

When she braids my hair, we'll sing
a happy song,
She speaks to me softly when I've
done something wrong.

Mom sees the future in a deck of colourful cards,
And she lets me play with her crystals and shards!

Actually, I shouldn't be
worried at all,
Most of the time, we're
having a ball!

What was I thinking, I'm not
in a pinch,
It's rather quite fun that my mom is
a witch!